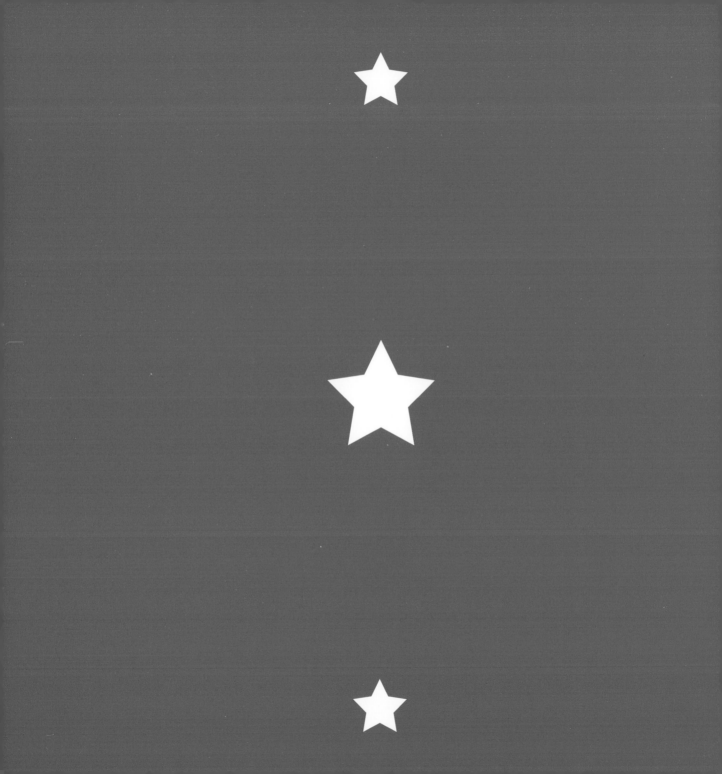

THE VERY FIRST CHRISTMAS

CATHERINE MACKENZIE

I remember your first Christmas. We said, 'You're here at last.' We had waited for our baby for sooo long.'

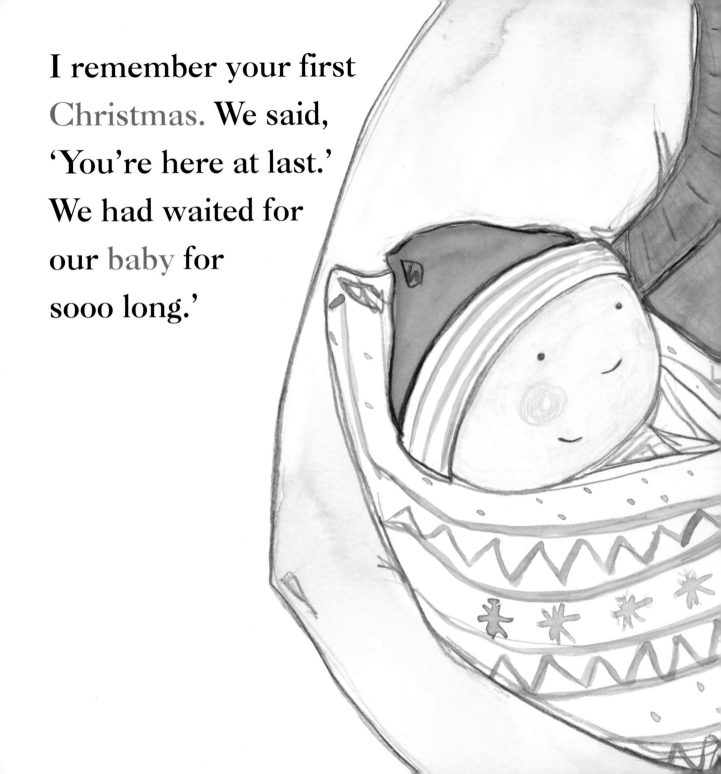

On the very first Christmas another baby was born in Bethlehem. His name was Jesus.

Jesus is the Son of God.

The world had waited
for Jesus, the Saviour,
for sooo long.

On your first Christmas we sent letters and cards. We told family and neighbours. 'Our baby is here'.

On the very first Christmas
the angels sang loudly,
'Joy to the world.
A Saviour is born.'

On your first Christmas
you slept in a crib
with a soft blanket.
It was lovely to have you
in our family, our very own
baby.

On the very first Christmas, God's Son, Jesus, slept in a box with straw for a bed.

On your first Christmas the visitors were excited to see our new baby. They cuddled you lots.

On the very first
Christmas shepherds
visited Bethlehem.
Angels had told them
the Saviour was there.

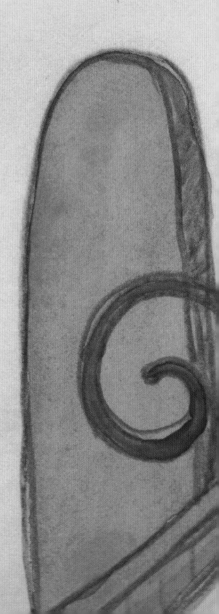

On your first Christmas you got presents.
There was wrapping paper everywhere!

On the very first Christmas
wise men came to worship Jesus. They gave
him gold, perfume and ointment.

On your first Christmas we took you for a walk. Everyone wanted to see our baby.

On the very first Christmas Jesus was taken to the temple. Simeon had been waiting to see the Saviour for sooo long! When he saw Jesus he gasped, 'I've seen salvation!'

You see, the very first Christmas is just part of the greatest gift ever. The baby in the manger became the Saviour on the Cross. Jesus!

He is the perfect Son of God who came to save his people from their sins.

A birth becomes a death – a death to end death. When we trust in Jesus Christ for forgiveness we will know real joy this Christmas.

CHRISTIAN FOCUS PUBLICATIONS

Christian Focus Publications publishes books for adults and children under its four main imprints: Christian Focus, CF4K, Mentor and Christian Heritage. Our books reflect our conviction that God's Word is reliable and Jesus is the way to know him, and live for ever with him. Our children's publication list includes a Sunday School curriculum that covers pre-school to early teens, and puzzle and activity books.

We also publish personal and family devotional titles, biographies and inspirational stories that children will love.

If you are looking for quality Bible teaching for children then we have an excellent range of Bible stories and age-specific theological books. From pre-school board books to teenage apologetics, we have it covered!

Find us at our web page: www.christianfocus.com

10 9 8 7 6 5 4 3 2 1
Copyright © Christian Focus Publications 2015
ISBN: 978-1-78191-608-7

Published by Christian Focus Publications,
Geanies House, Fearn, Tain, Ross-shire,
IV20 1TW, Scotland, U.K.

Cover design by Daniel van Straaten
Illustrations by Tessa Janes
Printed in China